Essential Stitch Guide

WHITEWORK

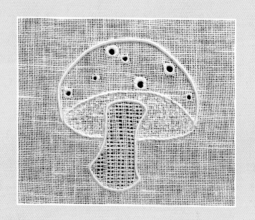

Essential Stitch Guide

WHITEWORK

LIZZY LANSBERRY

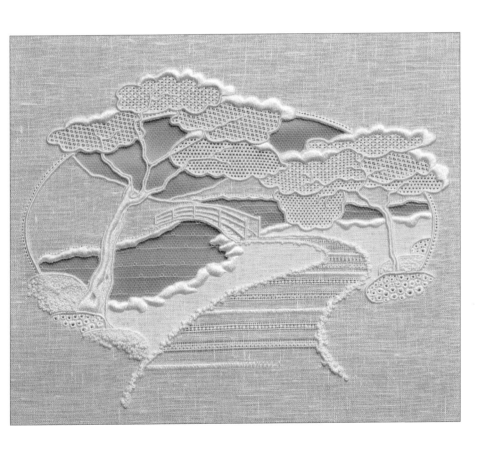

SEARCH PRESS

First published in Great Britain 2012
Search Press Limited
Wellwood, North Farm Road,
Tunbridge Wells, Kent TN2 3DR
Copyright © Lizzy Lansberry 2012
Photographs by Paul Bricknell at Search Press Studio
and by Gavin Sawyer, Roddy Paine
Photographic Studios
Photographs and design copyright
© Search Press Ltd. 2012
Photography of Hampton Court Palace with kind
permission from Historic Royal Palaces

ISBN: 978 1 84448 700 4

SUPPLIERS
If you have any difficulty obtaining any of the materials
and equipment mentioned in this book, please visit the
Search Press website: www.searchpress.com

For more details about the work of the Royal School
of Needlework, including courses, tours, our Studio,
tutors and where some of our work can be seen, please
go to our website: www.royal-needlework.org.uk

Printed in China

Page 1
Waterlily
*Worked by the author. The design and
inspiration for this piece are detailed on
pages 86–89.*

Page 2
Toadstool
*Worked by the author. This design features
outlines of trailing and stem stitch, with
details in random pulled thread eyelets,
seeding and drawn thread work.*

Page 3
Japanese Garden
*Worked by the author. This design, drawn
from the author's photograph of a Japanese-
style garden, includes all the techniques in
this book. It is shown in more detail on
pages 94–95.*

Above
Tulip
*Worked by the author. The flower is stitched
with pulled thread patterns. The background
has a pattern of drawn threads throughout,
and the piece is accented with trailing and
padded satin stitch. Also shown on page 71.*

Page 5
Autumn Maple Leaves
*Worked by the author. Also shown on
page 34.*

CONTENTS

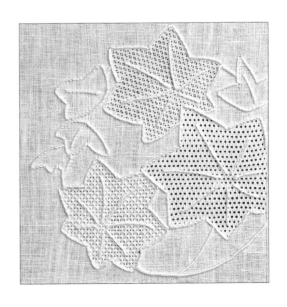

THE ROYAL SCHOOL OF NEEDLEWORK

The Royal School of Needlework was founded in 1872 by
Lady Victoria Welby because she wanted to ensure the arts
and techniques of high quality hand embroidery were
kept alive. At the time, Berlin wool work, a form of
canvaswork, was all the rage, almost to the exclusion of all
other techniques. The RSN began to train people in the
wide range of historic techniques from blackwork to silk
shading and from metal thread work to whitework. Working
with designers such as William Morris, Walter Crane and
Edward Burne-Jones, they created pieces for exhibitions in
the US and Paris, and for private commissions.

Since then, the RSN has used these techniques to make
new works for a wide variety of organisations from cathedrals
and synagogues to historic buildings and commercial
organisations as well as for individuals. We have also worked
for every British monarch since Queen Victoria.

Today, the RSN is at the forefront of teaching hand
embroidery techniques to the highest standard and welcomes
people from all over the world on to its courses every year.
We also have an extensive collection of embroidered textiles
and archival material which acts as a fantastic resource for
ideas and inspiration. Visitors to our rooms at Hampton
Court Palace, whether for classes or tours, can see
a changing range of works from the Collection on display.

While setting a high standard, the RSN exists to
encourage more people to participate in hand embroidery
and to this end, runs courses from beginner level in every
technique, for those who want to pursue embroidery as
a leisure interest, right through to our professional Certificate,
Diploma and Foundation Degree for those who want to
develop their future careers in embroidered textiles. While we
are trying to increase the number of locations where courses
are held, we are well aware that Hampton Court Palace, a few
other UK centres and San Francisco and Tokyo are not easily
accessible to many people who would like to explore

embroidery through the RSN approach, hence this series of Essential Stitch Guides.

Each book is written by an RSN Graduate Apprentice who has spent three years at the RSN learning techniques and then applying them in the RSN Studio, working on pieces from our Collection or on customers' contemporary and historic pieces. All are also tutors on our courses.

Alongside the actual stitches and historic examples of the technique you will also find a selection of works by the author and other RSN Apprentices and Students to show how a technique can really be used in new ways. While the RSN uses traditional stitch techniques as its medium, we believe that they can be used to create very contemporary works to ensure hand embroidery is not just kept alive, but flourishes into the future. We hope these images will inspire you to explore and develop your own work.

Opposite
and below

Hampton Court Palace,
Surrey, home of the
Royal School of Needlework.

INTRODUCTION

The word 'whitework' is an umbrella term, meaning pretty much any piece of needlework comprising white embroidery on white fabric. This means that any surface stitches done with only white could be referred to as whitework; but there are also a number of techniques that are specific to whitework. These are pulled thread work, counted satin stitch, drawn thread work, eyelets and cutwork. These techniques are all used to bring texture and tone to the design.

Typically both threads and fabric used for whitework are made from either cotton or linen fibres. Usually the fabric is evenly woven so that counted stitches may be worked, and within these criteria there are many options.

I have been stitching in one way or another all my life, and discovered whitework for the first time while studying Art & Design at college. I wrote a detailed study of cutwork, and the ideas lingered in my mind until I started the 'Basic Whitework' module in my second year of training at the RSN.

Since then I have loved whitework because it is incredibly versatile. That might sound surprising since it has no colour, but

Detail of a handkerchief from the author's own collection. It features a pretty combination of trailing, satin stitch, eyelets and tiny seeding stitches on a delicate cotton lawn. It may date from the early 19th century.

in fact that gives you freedom to tackle all sorts of designs – even those you might usually rule out because you don't like the colour. A good example of this is my Autumn Maple Leaves design on page 34. Orange and yellow are not really my colours, but the beautiful shapes lend themselves perfectly to whitework.

Whitework is all about the stitches – they have to do all the work, because there is no colour to distract the eye! For someone like me, who sees the world through a haze of stitches, this is perfect. I can take an image and translate it into a pattern of different stitches without concerning myself with colours. Unlike many other types of embroidery, whitework has almost unlimited stitches, which means you never get bored. Because the stitches are the stars, whitework really helps you to hone your needlework skills.

This book is by no means an exhaustive list of stitches, but it will help you to understand the principles involved, and you will see how to combine any or all of the fantastic techniques to suit your own style.

I hope that through this book you will discover the joy of whitework, and you will take the information and run with it in your own way.

Morris Inspired Cutwork

Worked by Jenny Adin-Christie. This piece of contemporary whitework demonstrates the versatility of the simple eyelet. The central flower motif is entirely separate from the fabric, simply supported by buttonhole bars.

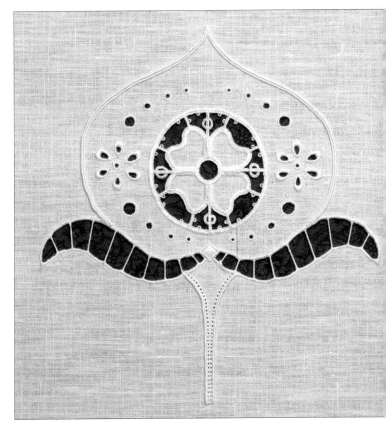

THE HISTORY OF WHITEWORK

The history of whitework is diverse and complicated, because there are so many techniques and cultures involved. In its many forms, it may be seen in historical textiles all over the world. In this book I have concentrated on the European traditions of whitework. The styles of whitework have seen external influences in design and technique, particularly from India since the 16th century, but trade within Europe seems to have had the greatest impact.

Pulled thread work means the use of counted stitches to pull apart the threads of the ground fabric, creating lace-like patterns. It can be found placed among surface stitches in many whitework pieces. There is speculation that it may have been used as early as 50BC on garments worn by Cleopatra of Egypt. Examples in Europe date from the 13th century and are most notably represented in Dresden work, a beautiful densely worked style of whitework developed in Germany, identified by the abundance of pulled thread fillings. This style gained popularity in the early 18th century as a substitute for lace. See examples on pages 45 and 63.

Surface stitches appear in combination with other techniques in every form of whitework and the most commonly used is satin stitch. Throughout its history, whitework designs have focused on natural forms such as flowers and leaves, for which surface stitches are perfect. In the early 19th century the local women of Ayrshire, Scotland, developed a highly skilled industry producing large volumes of a very detailed style of whitework known as Ayrshire work. It is known for its dense surface

Tablecloth

This is a charming example of intense stitching on a densely woven cloth. You can see that because of the nature of the fabric, the pulled thread areas create a lovely waffle texture, rather than a lacy pattern. The majority of the design is worked with satin stitch and trailing to create highly raised areas. The design itself, a symmetrical foliage pattern extending from the corners, could be from the 18th century.

stitching on very fine fabrics and is most often seen on christening robes and bonnets.

Eyelets are most frequently seen in a style known as Broderie Anglaise (originally a French term literally translating to English Embroidery), which was at its height in the late 19th century. This style uses both round and shaped eyelets to create patterns, with no other stitches required. It is useful as a means of decorating textiles that must withstand a lot of washing, and still reappears in summer fashion.

Drawn thread work uses a two-stage process to achieve a lace effect, and is thus distinguished from pulled thread work. Threads are removed from the ground fabric, and then the remaining threads and spaces are embroidered or woven. The earliest known example of drawn thread work was discovered in the 9th century tomb of Saint Cuthbert when it was opened in the early 12th century.

Cutwork is the name for the removal of areas of fabric, after securing the edges with stitching. Cutwork developed in its various forms all over Europe, but the most accomplished work came from Italy. The most famous style, Richelieu embroidery, is named after Cardinal Richelieu, who introduced it to France from Italy in the 16th century. It is identified by small loops on the buttonhole bars, known as picots. Cutwork became so popular in England in the 16th and 17th centuries that a law was passed allowing only the noble classes to wear it.

Whitework Border

Whitework can be used to create pretty borders and hems for clothing and table linens. This example shows a scalloped edging in buttonhole stitch with a repeated pattern of satin stitch flowers, eyelets and a little pulled thread work.

Counted Thread Sampler

This 1902 sampler of whitework stitches was probably made by a child learning to stitch. It shows a variety of wide drawn thread border patterns and two panels of pulled threads. The hem has been worked with hem stitch to give a dainty border.

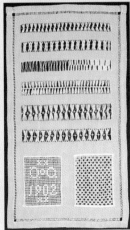

Materials & equipment

To work a beautiful piece of whitework embroidery, you will need a few basic supplies. To do your best work, it is essential that you are comfortable, and that you use good quality materials.

FRAMES

It is important that you use a sturdy frame for your embroidery to keep the stitch tension even and prevent puckering of the fabric. In whitework, there are some techniques which need to be worked under a great deal of tension, and others which require you to loosen the frame.

Slate frames

A slate frame is made up of two rollers and two arms, which fit together and give you very good control over the fabric tension. They come in various widths, and are ideal for medium-sized projects.

Slate frames may be held in place with a very strong floor clamp, but the sturdiest option is a set of trestles, which balance the frame at the desired angle.

Hoop frames

A hoop frame is ideal for small projects and for transporting easily. It is helpful to choose a frame with deep wooden hoops to hold the fabric securely. If possible, choose a style which allows you to use both hands to stitch, by using a clamp or stand to support the frame.

To allow the frame to grip the fabric tightly, and to prevent any marks on the fabric, it is a good idea to bind the frame with a strip of cotton tape or thin cotton. Wrap the tape around each hoop, at a slight angle so that it overlaps and covers the wood. Secure the ends with a few stitches, using strong thread.

As you work, remember to tighten the fabric every so often to keep it drum tight. Remove the fabric from the frame each time you stop working to prevent a hoop mark forming.

For whitework particularly, hoop frames can be useful for stitching patterns on very large pieces of cloth. It is not likely to be practical to keep a slate frame large enough for a tablecloth!

Trestles, a slate frame, hoop frames in various sizes and a seat clamp.

THREADS AND NEEDLES

Threads

Whitework uses quite a variety of different threads. The type of thread used depends on the technique, and it is therefore useful to have a selection.

I recommend using a length of no more than 25cm (10in) for whitework. This may seem excessively short, but because the thread is white it is very easy for it to become dirty. We rely on the texture of the thread, so it would not look good for it to become thin or fluffy.

Many of these threads are available in both white and off-white, and you should choose what you prefer – but make sure they all match! For this reason I try to buy as many of my threads as possible from the same brand so that the tones of white match well. There is no reason to choose any one brand over another; again it should be your own preference.

Stranded cotton
This is the dominant thread in most whitework designs. It can be used for any of the surface stitches, and gives a beautiful shine.

Coton à broder
This is a thicker thread that is quite soft, and not divisible. I usually use size 16, but it is available in other thicknesses. It may be used for surface stitches in the same way as stranded cotton to give a heavier, matt look. It is also very useful as padding for satin stitch or trailing.

Floche (soft cotton)
Also known as tapestry cotton, this thread is very thick and is made from slightly twisted strands of very soft fibres. It may be used for surface stitching on coarser work, but it can take practice to keep it under control. Its primary use is as padding for satin stitch and trailing.

Perlé cotton
This thread is very shiny and has a visible twist. It is available in a range of thicknesses and is useful for creating varied texture in a design alongside the other threads. It is suitable for surface stitches, and can also be used for larger scale drawn thread work.

Lace thread
Lace thread is a tightly spun thread that is very fine and very strong. It comes in a variety of thicknesses that create different effects. It is a good idea to begin with one of the thicker ones, and progress to the finest. A number denotes the thickness of the thread: the higher the number, the finer the thread.

Cotton or polyester machine thread
This is useful for tacking out areas of your design. You may use either white or light blue (either way it should be removed either as you work or afterwards).

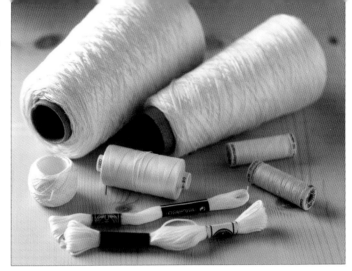

A selection of white threads.

Needles

Three different types of needle are needed for whitework. They each have their own particular purpose, so it is helpful to have a selection handy.

Tapestry
These needles have blunt points, which makes them perfect for any stitch where you do not want to pierce the threads of the fabric – pulled thread work, counted satin stitch and drawn thread work. The size chosen depends on the thickness of the thread – a larger eye for a thicker thread.

Crewel
Otherwise known as 'embroidery needles' these are slender needles with sharp points. The eye of the needle fits within the line of the needle, allowing for accurate work. They are used when working surface stitches with stranded cotton, coton à broder or lace thread. Again, the size depends on the thickness of the thread.

Chenille
These very sharp needles have a larger eye than crewel needles and are therefore suitable for surface stitching with the thicker threads. Their primary use in whitework is for padding with floche, or plunging thick threads when stitching trailing. I like to use a size 22, which is comfortable to thread and handle, as well as being accurate.

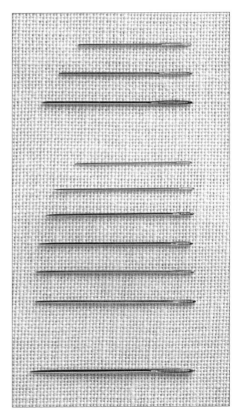

A selection of needles. From the top: tapestry needles sizes 28, 26 and 24; crewel needles sizes 12, 9, 8, 7, 6 and 5; chenille size 22.

15

FABRICS

Whitework is generally worked on an evenweave (or plain weave) fabric, where the number of threads per inch (TPI) is the same for both warp and weft. I always say you should buy the best you can afford, much as you might for clothing or furniture – after all, you are putting time and effort into your work, and you want it to be enjoyed long after you have finished it.

Evenweave linen is available in a range of TPI, from 20 to 55. It is also possible to get a cotton version in the heavier gauges. My preference for most of my projects is a 32 TPI Belfast linen. Natural slubs may appear in this type of fabric, but it is easy to count the threads.

Cotton or linen batiste (or batist) is a very fine, soft evenweave fabric which is tricky to count, but is beautiful when used for surface stitches, cutwork and eyelets.

Cotton or linen lawn is similar to batiste, but finer and more sheer. Again it is lovely for surface stitches, cutwork and eyelets. It may also be used for pulled and drawn thread work, but this may be tricky unless you have very good eyesight.

Cotton or linen muslin is a sheer fabric with a lower thread count than lawn. It is therefore easier to stitch pulled or drawn thread work. It is suitable for surface stitching, but be wary of using too much weighty thread as it will alter the drape of the fabric.

Dressmakers' net or tulle is used for net darning embroidered lace, which we will look at in the last chapter of this book.

Dragonfly

This design includes a number of surface stitches, including a counted satin stitch pattern in the lower wings. These are in contrast with the cutwork used in the upper wings; note where the buttonhole bars are placed to support the shapes. It is worked on 32 TPI Belfast linen to allow the counted stitch pattern to be seen easily. Cutwork on this gauge of linen is quite tricky, but achievable if worked very carefully.

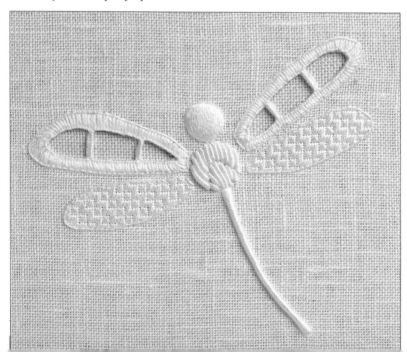

Evenweave linen fabric.

OTHER MATERIALS

To design your own projects you will need a sketchbook, tracing paper, pencils, fine black pen, coloured pencils, eraser, pencil sharpener, ruler and paper scissors. A light box also comes in very handy.

To prepare for working you will need dressmaker's scissors, acid free tissue paper, a tape measure and a permanent blue pencil. You may also need glass-headed pins, split pins, a bracing needle, parcel string and button thread.

I find it helpful to have a selection of embroidery scissors on hand. I use straight, curved and lace versions. Each has its own strengths, but if you cannot get the more specialist ones don't worry, straight embroidery scissors will do the job as long as you keep them sharp.

A magnifying glass can be a great help, particularly with the counted stitches – please don't be afraid to try one.

A mellor (or laying tool) can be useful for guiding threads without touching them too much.

A stiletto is used for making neat round eyelets without cutting the fabric.

Curved needles are handy for mounting your embroidery on a board for display.

Once your embroidery is finished, larger items may have to be folded for storage or washing, and a mini iron makes it much easier to press closely around the embroidery.

Opposite

The other materials used in whitework.

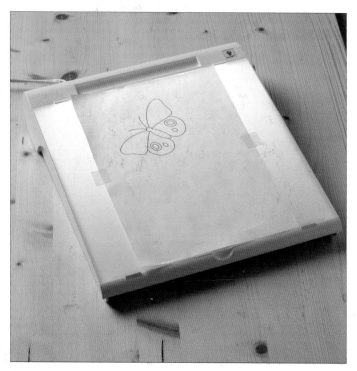

A light box, used for transferring the design.

18

DESIGN

How do we design for whitework, with no colour to work with? Whitework is all about tonal and textural contrast, and it is amazing what can be achieved with these two basic elements. It is important to remember which techniques are suitable for the shapes of your design and the kind of texture they will achieve – think about which areas you want to be prominent.

Also consider which techniques you can use together to be able to stitch most comfortably. For example, if you would like to include a lot of pulled thread work, you may wish to choose a coarser linen fabric, in which case cutwork would be difficult.

The following elements are covered in detail in this book. You may choose to use any combination of these techniques – as many or as few as you like.

Lovebirds

This design shows how the different elements can be combined. Note how the pulled thread, cutwork and eyelets really stand out when a dark backing is used. The birds' tails are both stitched in long and short, but the two angles look totally different. The curled stem is a simple stem stitch line, but worked in coton à broder to make it more prominent. The small satin stitch leaves catch the light at various angles.

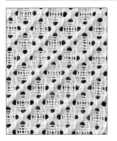

Open trellis filling.

PULLED THREAD WORK

Pulled thread work involves pulling the threads of the fabric tightly together to make a lacy pattern. There are a wide variety of patterns, each giving a different effect. It is very good for covering large areas with texture and is usually worked within an outlined shape, though it can be worked without an outline in some designs. You are pulling little holes in the fabric, so this can be used to give a darker tone to an area. As a counted stitch, you may find this easier on coarser evenweave linen, but it may be stitched on any fabric, even fine cotton lawn.

SATIN STITCH

Satin stitch is often the most raised part of a design because it can be very highly padded. It gives the design an area of high shine. The direction of the stitches can be angled so as to catch the light differently in different places, such as turning around a curve, to emphasize shapes. Satin stitch is suitable for shapes up to about 8mm (¼in) wide. It is easier to achieve very smooth edges on finer fabric, but with a good split stitch foundation, it may be worked on any fabric.

TRAILING

Usually trailing creates fairly narrow lines. The width can be varied quite a lot by the number of core threads. It can be worked in stranded cotton or coton à broder and it picks up the light very well, giving a shiny surface. Use trailing for outlines and design elements such as tendrils.

LONG AND SHORT

Long and short can be worked in stranded cotton or silk, which give a smooth, blended appearance. Changing the angle of the stitches around a curve will emphasise the shape. Long and short is a good way of filling almost any shape, including ones with wobbly edges that would be tricky in satin stitch.

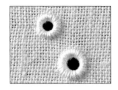

DECORATIVE STITCHES

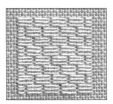

These add texture and life to a design by reflecting the light in different directions; stitches such as fishbone are a simple but attractive way to fill a leaf shape, and French knots may be used to fill any shape or size of space.

Counted satin stitch.

EYELETS

Eyelets are very useful design elements – a simple way to create high contrast. Worked in a variety of sizes and shapes, they can make a design in themselves, but they also combine very well with small satin stitch elements and trailing.

DRAWN THREAD WORK

Drawn thread work is most often seen in borders; used like this it can be a lovely way to finish off a design. You can also stitch drawn thread work within a design to create a striped pattern. Since this technique involves removing one thread at a time, it is easier on coarse linen, but it may be worked with care on any good, evenly woven fabric.

A woven wheel corner.

CUTWORK

Cutwork is suitable for shapes up to about 8mm (¼in) wide, such as leaf shapes or bands. It may be used on wider and more complex shapes if several buttonhole bars are used as supports. Remember that completely removing part of the fabric means you can see through to whatever is behind it, so choose any backing colour wisely. Since cutwork involves cutting into the fabric, a firm, closely woven fabric will give a stronger result. It is not recommended to try this on coarse linen, as the stitching may not be enough to protect the edges.

Cutwork with trailing.

21

DESIGNING A PIECE

So now we know what we have to work with. Remember, you don't have to use all the different elements in one design – and most importantly, don't panic! If you are not used to designing your own work, start small. You will soon build the confidence to take on bigger projects. Try copying a historical piece – there is plenty out there to inspire you. A good way to get started is to trace ideas on to paper, cut them out and rearrange them until you like the result.

Begin by taking an image or pattern that inspires you, or simply doodle away until you come up with something you like. It is always handy to have a sketchbook around for those moments of inspiration when you are out and about, or in the middle of the night! I find the easiest way to design is to take a photograph, or a simple sketch, and work from there with tracing paper, or my trusty computer.

For this butterfly, I looked at a photograph my Dad took of a beautiful peacock butterfly (right). I first made a sketch of the butterfly, marking the placement of the details on the wings. I knew I wanted the wings to be relatively symmetrical so I dispensed with some of the perspective in the photograph to flatten out the image.

Photograph by Peter Lansberry.

I scanned the image into my computer and used image manipulation software to create a clear outline. I then created a simplified version by moving the elements around and evening out the curves. You can do the same thing by using tracing paper. Try tracing different elements separately and cutting them out. Then arrange them on a piece of paper until you are happy with the design, and retrace the final outline on a new sheet.

Once I have a clear outline to work with I create drawings of the design, trying out different stitch effects.

My sketch.

The clear outline of the design.

22

Think about which areas would suit different stitches, and try to lightly sketch in a rough idea of the texture, for example cross-hatching gives the impression of pulled thread work. Colour any areas that are unstitched (including the background) with a very light tone, so that the white stitched areas stand out.

If I am including satin stitch or long and short in my design, I create another drawing showing the angle of the stitches. For cutwork areas I sketch in where I think any buttonhole bars will be needed for support.

When you are happy with the result, you are ready to transfer your design and frame up your fabric, and you can work out a stitch plan. Don't forget that as long as you have an outline you like, some elements of the design can change as you go along.

Lastly, think about a background colour. Whether it is a framed artwork or a draped tablecloth, the colour showing through makes a great difference to the overall effect. Throughout this book I have used blue backgrounds, because blue makes the work look clean and white. Other colours may also work well – a cherry red can be beautiful for example. I would advise being wary of yellow, orange and yellow-greens as they are likely to make the work look discoloured. Hold various colours behind the work and see what you like best.

My computer drawing of the design, including ideas for stitching.

The finished embroidery.

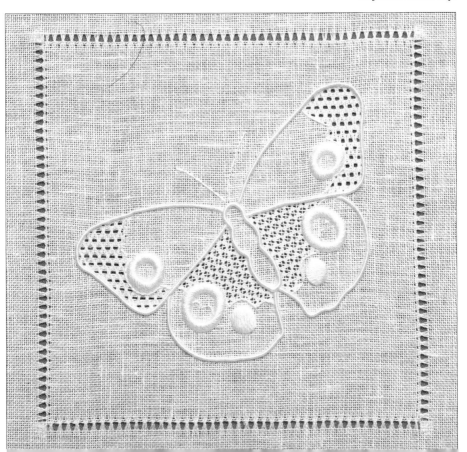

THE ORDER OF WORK

Before you start to stitch, it is important to plan the order of work. Although there is a degree of flexibility, particularly in the early stages, it is useful to have a guide so that you don't end up in a mess.

With whitework there are some fairly clear guidelines, based on what effect each type of stitch has on the fabric. Some stitches add strength and some take it away; some stitches are flat, some are raised.

1. PULLED THREAD WORK

This comes first because it is flat, so it needs to be complete before any raised stitching is done.

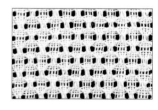

Honeycomb darning.

2. CORE SURFACE STITCHES

Generally it is a good idea to work outlines first, and then any solid areas. This is also the time to work the stitching of cutwork (method 2 – see page 79), but do not cut them yet!

Turned satin stitch.

3. DECORATIVE SURFACE STITCHES

These are often used to fill an area so it is good to stitch these after any outlines are complete.

French knots.

4. EYELETS

Eyelets create small details and the placement may be dependent on other parts of the design so you should work them after all the surface stitching is complete.

Shaped eyelets.

5. DRAWN THREAD WORK

This is a delicate process and should be worked after all the surface stitches and eyelets are finished. If it is used for a border, it is easier to position it at this stage. Stretch the fabric only once more after this to embroider on the remaining threads.

Double twist.

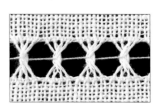

---

6. CUTWORK

This is the time to finish off the work by releasing the fabric from the frame and trimming any cutwork areas. After this is complete, it would not be a good idea to stretch the fabric in a frame.

Cutwork with buttonhole stitch.

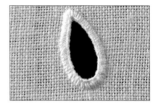

Pulled thread

Long and short, core

Drawn thread border

Stem stitch, decorative

Satin stitch, core

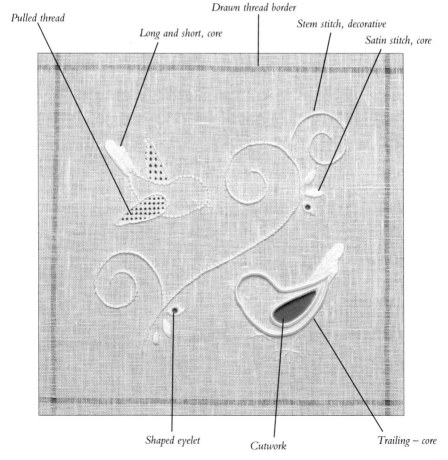

Shaped eyelet

Cutwork

Trailing – core

FRAMING UP

For most whitework, the fabric should be kept taut. This helps to prevent puckering and keeps the tension of the stitches even. Hoop frames are useful for small projects. Some techniques require you to loosen and re-tighten the fabric: a slate frame is ideal because the tension can be adjusted gradually.

AN EMBROIDERY HOOP

Before framing up with a hoop, make sure that the two hoops fit snugly together (not so tight that they are difficult to pull apart, but not so loose that they separate on their own).

1 Cover a flat surface with tissue paper. Put the outer hoop down on the surface and place the fabric over it with the design face down. Try to line up the design with the middle of the hoop, as this is where the fabric will be at the best tension.

2 Line up the inner ring over the outer ring, with the fabric in between.

3 Press down hard on the inner ring, trapping the fabric. I usually stand up to do this, as it is much easier with more weight behind your arms.

4 If there are still some wrinkles or 'bubbles' in the fabric, ease them out by pulling the edges of the fabric with your hands. Ensure that the frame remains drum tight while you are stitching.

A SLATE FRAME

This consists of four separate pieces of wood, two rollers (with webbing attached) and two arms (which have holes in for the pegs). The fabric is stitched into the frame and then tightened to a drum-like tension. If the fabric becomes slack as you work, you can re-tighten using the string at the sides, or by moving a peg to the next hole. The frame rests on top of trestles, which you can comfortably sit at to stitch.

1 Measure each roller from the inside edge of the arm slots and mark the centre of the webbing with a pencil. Fold over 1cm (³/₈in) at the top and bottom of the fabric, on the grain. Match up the centre of the fabric with the centre of the webbing.

2 Pin the fabric to the webbing, with the 1cm (³/₈in) fold facing the webbing. Pin from the centre to each end, placing the pins at right angles to the webbing.

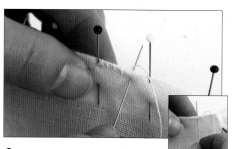

3 Thread a sharp needle with a length of strong button thread and make a knot in the end of the thread. Beginning in the centre, take the needle through the fabric a few threads in from the edge. Oversew through the linen and webbing a few times to secure the thread. Then continue stitching tightly to each end, with the stitches 2–3mm (¹/₈in) apart, removing pins as you go. At the end, stitch back for about 2cm (³/₄in) and oversew to secure the thread. Repeat at the other end of the fabric.

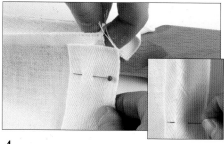

4 Decide how much fabric needs to be exposed, and roll in the rollers accordingly. Place the arms in the frame and put a peg in the same hole either side to hold the fabric steady. Cut a piece of webbing to fit the side of the fabric. Place it three-quarters on the fabric with a quarter overhanging the edge and pin it in place. Secure it to the linen with strong button thread using a basting stitch (a long diagonal stitch on the front, with a horizontal straight stitch on the back as shown). Do this on both sides.

5 Move the pegs in the arms so that the fabric is stretched tight. Thread a bracing needle with parcel string, straight from the ball. Take the bracing needle down through the webbing (never bring the needle up towards you, it is very sharp). Take it around the arm of the frame and back through the webbing at 2.5cm (1in) intervals. Do this on both sides.

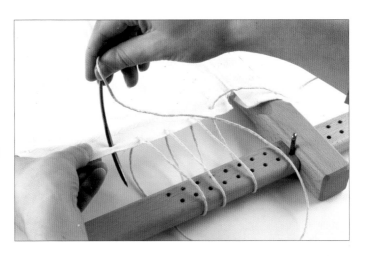

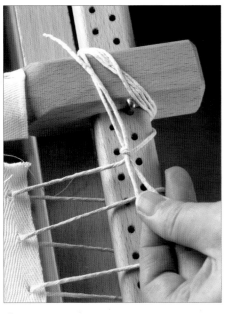

6 Make sure there is a good length of excess string on both ends before cutting. Wind the excess on one end around the end of the frame as shown and tie the end in a secure way (a slip knot is good, as it is easily released later).

7 Starting from the secure end, work along the frame tightening the string. Begin by tightening a little, then switch to the other side. Tightening the frame gradually avoids distorting the grain. If necessary, once the string is tight, rest the frame upright on the floor and use the sole of your foot to press down on each end of the bottom roller. Move the pegs one by one to increase the tension in the fabric.

TRANSFERRING A DESIGN

For most designs, the best and simplest method of transferring is to trace the outline directly on to the fabric. When this is not appropriate, the tacking method is used.

Light box method

1 Tape the design to the light box and switch it on. If you do not have a light box, a very clean window is not a bad substitute.

2 Position your fabric over the design and tape it in place. Use a very sharp pencil to trace the design on to the fabric. Draw with light, feathery strokes to gradually build up the outline – remember it is easy to add to the lines, but very hard to remove them! A permanent blue pencil is a great tool for this – the blue colour will not distract from your work even if you do not quite manage to cover the lines, and it will not bleed through if you decide to wash your embroidery.

Tacking method

There are times when a pencil line will not be the best method – for example where it would not be covered with stitching. This particularly applies to drawn thread work, and can also be useful if you plan to add details over pulled work.

To mark a border: thread a small tapestry needle with machine thread (here I have used white on the blue linen, but a light blue thread is good on white linen). Tie a knot in the end of the thread and run a line of long stitches along where you wish to place the border. Try marking out the centre of each line with a pin to gauge the distance from the design.

To mark other design lines: trace the design lightly on to a piece of tissue paper. Tack the tissue paper in place on the fabric (over any embroidery you have already done). With a sharp needle threaded with machine thread, use long stitches to mark the design lines, taking the needle through both tissue and fabric. Once complete, tear away the tissue paper.

All tacking lines should be removed as you work the embroidery.

To indicate where a border will go, lines have been marked with long stitches in contrasting thread, using a tapestry needle.

GETTING STARTED

COVERING YOUR WORK

It is always important to keep your embroidery clean, but especially so with whitework. With no colour to distract the eye, a small stain can be very obvious. While working, try to keep as much of the work covered as possible. For long-term storage and transport, I recommend wrapping the whole thing in tissue paper and an old (but clean) white sheet or cloth.

1 Frame up as on pages 26–27, but with tissue paper between the fabric and the outer ring. Carefully make a hole in the tissue with a pin (this avoids getting sharp scissors near your fabric).

2 You can now tear away a piece of tissue paper to expose just the part of the design you are about to start stitching. As you work, either tear away a bit more tissue paper or simply reposition it when you take the fabric out of the frame. Remember to keep another piece of tissue paper handy to cover the whole thing when you take a tea break.

In a slate frame

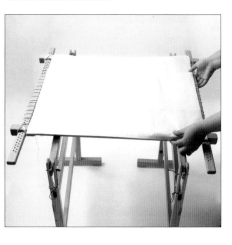

1 Use low-tack sticky tape to attach a double layer of tissue paper to each roller.

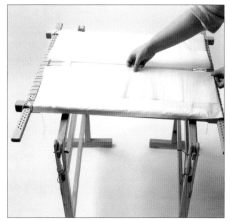

2 Fold back the sheets to expose a strip of fabric, including the area you are going to begin working.

3 Fold two more sheets of tissue paper into strips and slot them underneath the first two, leaving only a very small area exposed. Pin all the tissue paper in place. When you take a break, pin another double layer of tissue paper over the exposed area.

Stitches

The following pages show the fundamental stitches of whitework. They are divided by technique, and displayed in the order they should be worked. Some stitches are shown on blue fabric so that you can clearly see the threads. As for most types of embroidery, you should generally cast on with two little stitches in an area that will later be covered.

PULLED THREAD STITCHES

Pulled thread work is used to create lacy patterns in the fabric, without removing any threads. The thread used should match the thickness of the grain of the fabric. The following pages take you through the steps of each pattern.

When the directions say to 'pull', this means that you need to give a short, sharp tug on the thread, in the direction of the stitch. This is generally each time you bring the needle up through the fabric. You will see that doing this creates little holes in the fabric, which will build into a lacy pattern. It is important to pull consistently on the fabric so that the pattern will be even; the best way to do this is to get into a rhythm.

Try to begin an area across the widest point, considering which angle the pattern is worked at (some are straight across, others are diagonal). When working within an area, you will need to break up the pattern when you reach the edge. None of your stitches should go over the border, and the end of each row should be tied off with a couple of tiny holding stitches on the border. Sometimes it is helpful to put 'fake' stitches at the edge, which are not pulled tight but complete the look of the pattern.

Note that these stitches are shown worked in one direction, but you may work them in whichever direction you find most comfortable, or which suits the shape.

Autumn Maple Leaves

This piece shows three pulled thread stitches: diagonal drawn filling, wave stitch and honeycomb darning (clockwise from top). The outline details are stitched with stem stitch and trailing.

PREPARATION

The shape should be outlined with double running stitch to firmly enclose the area. This helps to prevent the surrounding linen from being distorted.

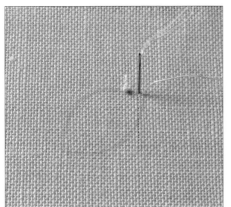

1 Thread a length of lace thread into a small crewel needle and tie a knot in the end. Cast on with two little stitches on the line.

2 Make running stitches round the line. These should be around 2mm (⅛in) long, with gaps of the same length. Wherever possible, try to split the threads of the fabric rather than going through the holes.

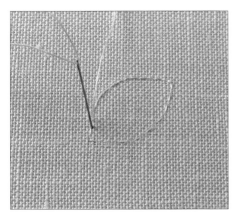

3 Go back around the line, filling in the gaps to make double running stitch.

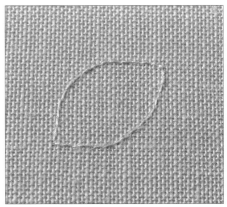

The design prepared for pulled thread work, with a double running stitch outline.

HONEYCOMB DARNING

Honeycomb darning is a simple pulled thread pattern that is worked in horizontal rows. As the name suggests, it creates a honeycomb pattern. Try this with thicker lace thread for a raised effect.

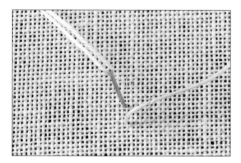

1 Bring the needle up just inside your outline. Make a vertical stitch up over four threads.

2 Make a horizontal stitch under four threads, to the left.

3 Pull to the left, against the last stitch.

4 Make a vertical stitch down over four threads.

5 Make a horizontal stitch under four threads to the left, and pull again. Repeat to complete your first row.

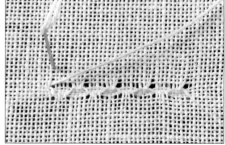

6 Make a holding stitch in the border and then bring the needle out of the first hole on the top of the previous row. Take a vertical stitch up over four threads to begin the new row.

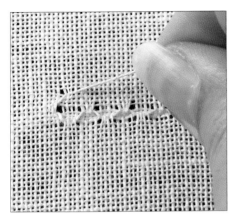 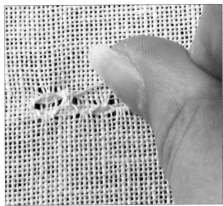

7 Make a horizontal stitch under four threads to the right, and pull.

8 Make a vertical stitch down over four threads, taking the needle down through the hole of the previous row. Bring the needle up four threads to the right, through the next hole along, and pull again. Repeat to complete the row.

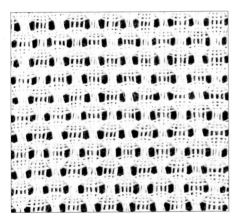

An example of honeycomb darning.

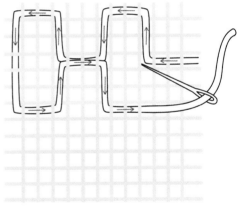

Diagram

Note

To make sure the pattern is correct, turn the embroidery over. On the back you will see that the horizontal stitches are doubled up.

WAVE STITCH

Like honeycomb darning, wave stitch is worked in
horizontal rows. This one is a bit trickier to stitch evenly,
but can be very useful and is good for small areas.

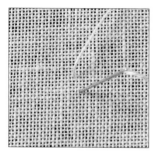

1 Bring the needle up two
threads inside your outline. Count
right two and down four and take
the needle down.

2 Count left four, bring the
needle up and pull to the left.

3 Take the needle back
through the first hole (right two
and up four).

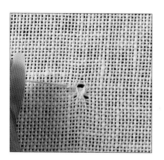

4 Count left four, bring the needle
up and pull. Repeat to complete
the first row.

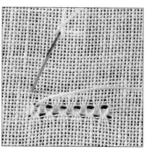

5 To begin the next row, bring
the needle out of the first top
hole of the previous row. Count
left two and up four and take the
needle down.

6 Count right four, bring the
needle up and pull to the right.

 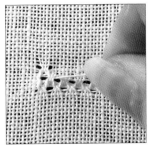

7 Count left two and down four and take the needle down in the hole of the previous row.

8 Count right four (to the next hole of the previous row), bring the needle up and pull. Repeat to complete each row.

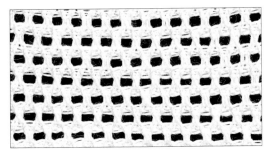

An example of wave stitch.

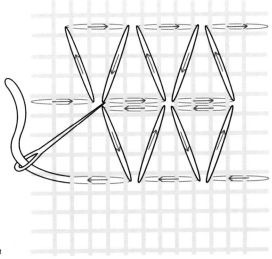

Diagram

FOUR-SIDED STITCH

Four-sided stitch looks as though it has a lot of steps, but it is really just a case of repeating squares. It creates a very even pattern of little holes, and is great for borders.

 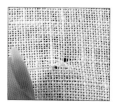 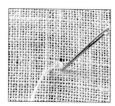 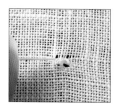

1 Bring the needle up just inside your outline. Make a vertical stitch up over four threads.

2 Count left four and down four and bring the needle up, making a diagonal stitch underneath. Pull to the left.

3 Make a horizontal stitch four to the right, taking the needle down in the first hole.

4 Count left four and up four and bring the needle up, making a diagonal stitch underneath, and pull.

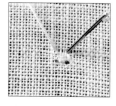   

5 Make a horizontal stitch four to the right, taking the needle down in the top right hole.

6 Count left four and down four, bring the needle up in the bottom left hole, and pull.

7 Make a vertical stitch up over four threads. This becomes the first stitch of the next square. Repeat to complete the row.

8 Count four threads up from the top left hole of the previous row and bring the needle up. Make a vertical stitch over four threads down to the hole to make the first stitch. Work the row in the same way as the first row, but in reverse.

An example of four-sided stitch.

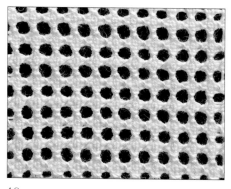

Diagram

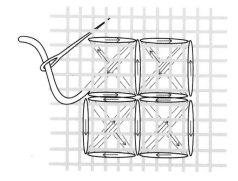

SINGLE FAGGOT STITCH

Single faggot stitch is a simple stitch worked on the diagonal. It is the foundation for a variety of diagonal stitches.

 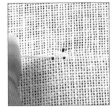  

1 Bring the needle up just inside your outline. Make a vertical stitch up over four threads.

2 Count left four and down four, bring the needle up and pull.

3 Make a horizontal stitch four to the right, back down into the first hole.

4 Count four left and four down, bring the needle up and pull.

5 Make a vertical stitch up over four threads, into the previous hole. Repeat to complete the first row.

6 To begin the second row, bring the needle up through the first hole of the previous row and make a horizontal stitch over four threads to the left.

7 Count right four and up four, bring the needle up and pull.

8 Make a vertical stitch down over four threads, into the hole of the previous row. Repeat to complete the row.

An example of single faggot stitch.

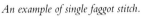
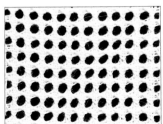

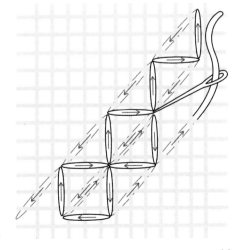

Diagram

DIAGONAL DRAWN FILLING

Diagonal drawn filling is based on single faggot stitch, worked on the diagonal.
The steps are the same as for single faggot stitch, but the rows are spaced one
thread apart. It creates a pretty pattern that is one of my favourites.

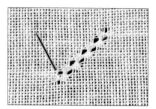

1 For the first row, follow the steps for single faggot stitch on page 41. Instead of bringing the needle up in the first hole of the previous row, move it one thread up and one thread to the left.

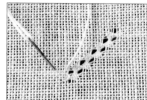

2 Make a horizontal stitch over four threads to the left.

3 Count up four and right four, bring the needle up and pull.

4 Make a vertical stitch down over four threads, into the previous hole of this row.

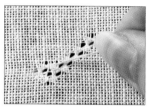

5 Count right four and up four, bring the needle up and pull. Notice that when you pull this time, you open up a hole with a cross shape inside it (it looks a bit like a window).

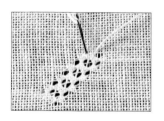

6 Repeat to complete the row.

An example of diagonal drawn filling.

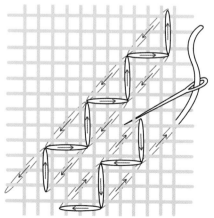

Diagram

DIAGONAL CROSS FILLING

Diagonal cross filling creates a neat pattern with raised stripes. Try stitching it with a thick lace thread to enhance the stripes, or with a fine thread to keep it flat.

 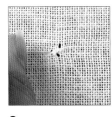 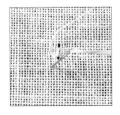 

1 Bring the needle up just inside your outline. Make a vertical stitch down over six threads.

2 Count left three and up three, bring the needle up and pull. This makes a small diagonal stitch on the back.

3 Make a vertical stitch down over six threads. Repeat along the row.

4 At the end of the row, count left three and up three from the last hole and bring the needle up. Make a horizontal stitch to the right over six threads to form a cross.

   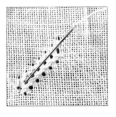

5 Count left three and up three, bring the needle up in the next hole of the previous row and pull. Repeat to complete the row.

6 To start the next row, count up six threads from the first hole of the previous row and bring the needle up. Make a vertical stitch down over six threads into the first hole of the previous row.

7 Count left three and up three, bring the needle up and pull. Repeat along the row.

8 At the end of the row, repeat step 4 to complete the second row. Repeat to fill the shape.

Diagram

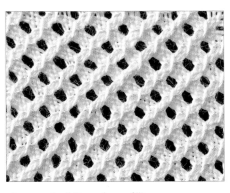

An example of diagonal cross filling.

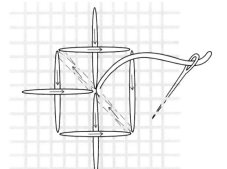

OPEN TRELLIS FILLING

Open trellis filling is a lovely stitch based on diagonal cross filling. It is suitable for large areas.

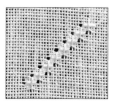  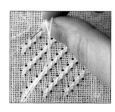

1 For the first row, follow the steps for diagonal cross filling on page 43.

2 For the second row, again follow the steps for diagonal cross filling, but leave a space between the rows. From the first hole of the first row, count down six threads and begin the second row. Fill the shape with these evenly spaced rows.

3 The next rows are worked in the same way, but from top left to bottom right, crossing the first rows. Bring the needle up in the top left corner, through the first hole of a row. Make a vertical stitch down over six threads, over the previous cross.

 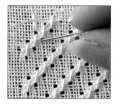  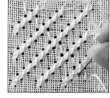

4 Count right three and up three, bring the needle up and pull.

5 Make a vertical stitch down over six threads. Repeat along the row.

6 At the end of the row, count right three and up three from the last hole, and bring the needle up. Make a horizontal stitch to the left over six threads, down into the next hole, to form a cross. Repeat to complete the row.

7 Begin the next row, leaving a space between the rows. From the first hole, count down six threads and begin the next row. Fill the shape with these evenly spaced rows.

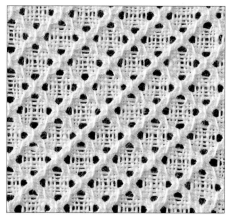

An example of open trellis filling.

Dresden Work

Detail of an embroidered border in the Dresden style. It features a variety of pulled thread patterns combined with counted satin patterns and flat satin stitch details, stitched on very fine cotton lawn.

EYELETS

Pulled work eyelets may be worked individually or combined to form a pattern. There are various different shapes to choose from. The method is the same for each, only the placement of the stitches changes (see diagrams).

Round eyelets

1 Bring the needle up and make a horizontal stitch four threads to the left (this is the position of the centre hole).

2 Bring the needle up one thread below the starting point and pull.

3 Take the needle down in the centre hole (four threads left and one up).

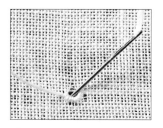

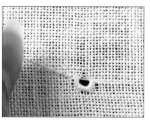

4 Follow the diagram for the placement of the stitches, and continue round the eyelet.

5 Pull the thread each time you bring the needle up through the fabric, to maintain a neat hole.

6 Pull the final stitch.

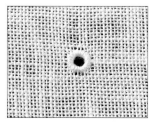

The finished eyelet.

Diagram

Small round eyelet

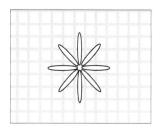

Diagram

The finished small round eyelet.

Diamond eyelet

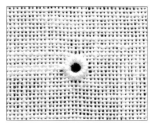

The finished diamond eyelet.

Square eyelet

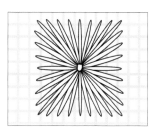

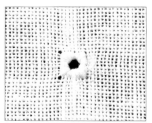

The finished square eyelet.

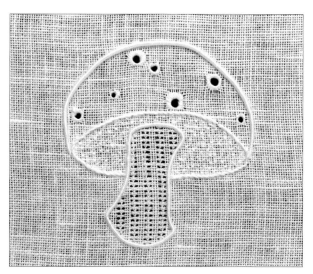

This toadstool design makes use of pulled work eyelets. Each eyelet is a different size and shape to give a natural appearance.

COMBINING PULLED THREAD STITCHES

Many of the pulled thread stitches can be combined to create interesting patterns. Try experimenting with the stitches to create your own patterns.

Single faggot stitch with diagonal cross filling

Both stitches are diagonal so they combine easily. To make the stitches fit neatly together, sometimes you need to change the count. Because the diagonal cross filling is counted over six threads, the single faggot stitch has been reduced to three instead of four: two times three makes six, so the two fit together.

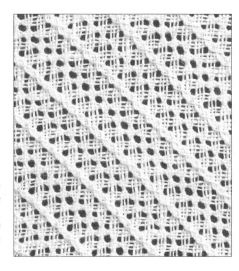

The pattern is worked as follows: two rows of single faggot stitch, a space of three threads, one row of diagonal cross filling, a space of three threads, one row of single faggot stitch, one row of diagonal cross filling, and so on.

Four-sided stitch with square eyelets

Square eyelets work well counted over eight threads, and four-sided stitch counted over four threads fits in well.

The pattern is worked as follows: one vertical row of four-sided stitch, a space of two threads, a vertical row of square eyelets (with no spaces in between), a space of two threads, and so on.

CORE SURFACE STITCHES

These stitches are essential to whitework. They give weight to the design by providing solid areas of stitch. They can be worked with stranded cotton, coton à broder or perlé cotton.

SPLIT STITCH

Any area of satin stitch or long and short should have an outline of split stitch; it gives a firm foundation to the stitch so that an even tension is maintained and the fabric is not distorted. It really helps to give a lovely smooth edge to any shape.

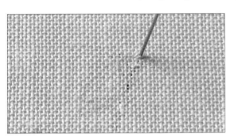

1 Make a stitch and come up halfway along it, splitting the thread.

2 Continue in the same way.

3 To turn a corner, come up a stitch length away from the corner and make a back stitch.

4 Split the back stitch and go down again to continue.

The finished split stitch outline.

Diagram

BASIC SATIN STITCH

Once you have mastered this simple stitch, you can tackle all sorts of
designs. In some ways, although this is the most basic version, it can be
the most difficult because you have to be very careful to keep the angle of
the stitches consistent.

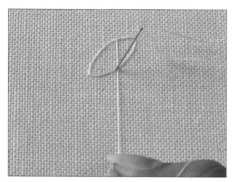

1 Beginning halfway along one side, bring the
needle up just outside the split stitch outline. Hold the
thread to set the angle of the first stitch, and take the
needle down accordingly, just outside the split stitch.

2 Bring the needle up on the first side, very close
to the first stitch, just outside the split stitch. Make
a second stitch, angling the needle towards the
previous stitch and towards the split stitch.

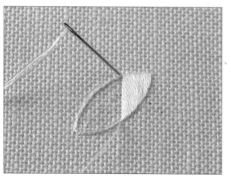

3 Work outwards towards the end of the shape, and
then begin again in the middle. This time bring the
needle up on the other side of the shape, and angle
the needle towards the previous stitch as before.

The design worked in basic satin stitch.

Diagram of stitch direction.

TURNED SATIN STITCH

This is a very useful stitch because the changing angles reflect light in a very interesting way. The turned stitches allow for almost any shape to be worked.

1 Outline the shape with split stitch and fill with any padding required (pages 52–53). Bring the needle up just outside the split stitch outline part way along the shape. Choose the required angle and take the needle down accordingly, just outside the split stitch.

2 Bring the needle up on the first side again, very close to the first stitch, just outside the split stitch. Make a second stitch, angling the needle towards the previous stitch and towards the split stitch.

3 Continue to stitch in this way to cover the shape. To change the angle gradually as you move along the shape, bring the needle up even closer to the previous stitch on the inside curve and take it down a little further away on the outside curve.

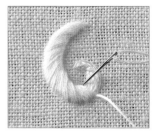

4 Complete the first half of the shape with a last neat stitch. Try to think about the angles in advance so that when you get to this stitch, it will easily cover the outline.

5 Begin again in the middle. As for basic satin stitch, you will reverse the direction of the stitches.

6 This time to change the angle, bring the needle up a little further away from the previous stitch on the outside curve and tuck it even closer on the inside curve.

The finished example of turned satin stitch. The angles will be different for each shape that you stitch, so try to have a rough plan of what you want it to look like before you start.

PADDED SATIN (SATIN STITCH VARIANT)

This version of padded satin stitch gives a smooth, rounded effect that is raised more in the centre of the shape and tapered towards the edges. Each layer of padding should be at a different angle, and the top layer should be at right angles to the satin stitch itself. There is no particular limit to the number of layers; it is determined by the size of the shape.

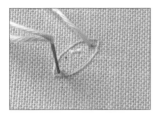

1 Outline the shape with split stitch first. Using a thick thread, bring the needle up a bit inside the split stitch outline. Make the first stitch across the longest part of the shape.

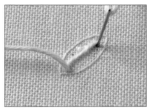

2 Bring the needle up close to the first stitch, at the same end, and make another stitch. Continue outwards to the edge.

3 Start again in the middle and complete the layer.

4 Work the next layer of padding at a different angle to the first, starting in the middle and working outwards. Start again in the middle and work outwards to complete the layer.

5 Stitch the third layer in the same way at another angle.

6 Work satin stitch with your chosen thread following the steps for basic satin stitch on page 48.

The finished design in padded satin (satin stitch).

PADDED SATIN (SPLIT STITCH VARIANT)

This version of padded satin stitch is a little more advanced. You need to be careful to keep a smooth surface on the padding to support the satin stitch. Because the layers are built up gradually, it allows for variation within one shape. You can work as many layers as you like, varying them according to the width of the shape and the desired height of the padding.

Here I have worked a leaf shape in two halves, to demonstrate the different levels of padding.

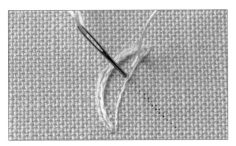

1 Outline the left-hand side with split stitch first. Using a thick thread, stitch a line of split stitches just inside the split stitch outline. The stitches should be 5–8mm (¼ –½in) long. Then continue the line around the shape, spiralling in towards the centre.

2 Add second and third layers of split stitch, continuing to spiral around the shape.

3 Work satin stitch over the padding, following the steps for turned satin stitch on page 51.

4 Outline the right-hand side with split stitch and then work split stitch padding inside it as before. This time stitch only one layer.

The finished design. The right-hand side is less padded than the left, giving it a flatter look.

LONG AND SHORT STITCH

Use long and short stitch to create areas of strong white. You can change the angle of the stitches to give flowing lines. The stitch length can vary depending on the shape; shorter lengths are useful to turn around tight curves and the maximum length is about 10mm (³⁄₈in).

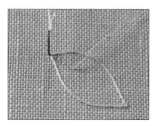

1 Work the outline in split stitch. Bring the needle up inside the shape and make the first stitch, going over the split stitch. For pointed shapes such as this leaf, extend the stitch slightly past the tip to create a sharp point.

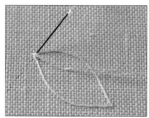

2 Make the next stitch just to one side of the first, bringing the needle up in the shape and angling it in towards the previous stitch and towards the split stitch.

3 Work stitches of varied lengths (make the lengths as random as possible) from the middle out towards the edge of the shape, then start again in the middle. This forms the first row.

4 Begin the second row, bringing the needle up, splitting the first stitch and overlapping about two-thirds of its length. Make a long stitch. Work across the row, extending each stitch. On a shape such as this leaf, the stitches are slightly angled towards the centre.

5 Add stitches on the edge as you continue, making sure that whenever you cross the edge, you take the stitch out over the edge and angle the needle towards the split stitch as for the first row.

6 Repeat until the shape is filled.

Opposite
White Peacock

Stitched by Sophie Long. This beautiful design of a stylized peacock makes brilliant use of long and short stitch – the whole body is filled with long and short, using the direction of the stitches to emphasise the shape. Swathes of satin stitch add highlights. Note the contrast between these shiny surface stitches and the patterned techniques in the peacock's tail.

TRAILING

Trailing is a very useful stitch, brilliant for creating outlines. It has a lovely shiny surface that reflects a lot of light, and the width can be adjusted to give very fine or bold lines. Use stranded cotton for the stitching for accuracy. I suggest beginning with at least three floche or six coton à broder threads for the core while you practise, then progress to finer or bolder trailing.

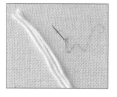 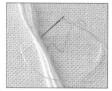 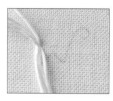 

1 Begin partway along the line, preferably on quite a straight section. Decide how many threads to use as the core. Bring the needle up just to one side of the line.

2 Bring the needle over the core threads and take it down just on the other side of the line. The stitch should be at right angles to the line. Pull fairly tightly on the first stitch and maintain the tension as you work the next stitch (after this you can relax a bit).

3 For each subsequent stitch, bring the needle up from underneath the core threads and take it down underneath them. The stitches should be as close together as you can manage, so as not to let any of the core threads show through.

4 As you turn a corner, change the angle of the stitches so they stay at right angles to the line at all times. They will be spaced a little further apart on the outside curve and even closer together on the inside curve.

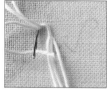 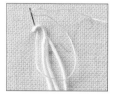 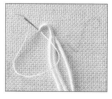 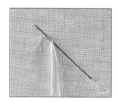

5 To finish a line, stop stitching just before the end of the line. Thread one of the core threads into a large chenille needle and take the needle down at the end of the line to plunge the thread through.

6 Repeat for the rest of the core threads and then continue to stitch, holding the core threads out of the way on the back.

7 Finish stitching to the end of the line, angling the needle out from under the core threads and back underneath them with each stitch.

8 If the trailing finishes away from any other stitching, turn to the back to cast off. Run the needle underneath the last few stitches, pull the thread through and trim.

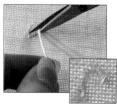 

9 On the back, trim the core threads as close as possible to the fabric so that no shadows will show on the front. Trim each thread individually for the neatest result.

A finished example.

Diagram

TAPERED TRAILING

Tapered trailing does exactly what it says on the tin: it is trailing, but tapered. With this method, you can go from any number of core threads down to nothing. In this leaf design I worked the outline with stem stitch and the stem with tapered trailing, starting with three floche threads.

1 Begin trailing as before. To gradually taper the line, separate the core threads (with floche you can divide the strands).

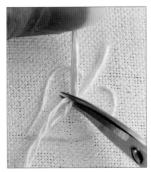

2 Lift the top threads out of the way and carefully snip a few of the strands closest to the fabric.

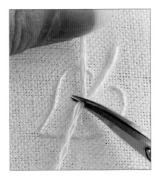

3 Continue to stitch over the remaining core threads, making sure no fluff shows where the threads were cut. Then repeat the trimming process as many times as necessary.

4 Finish the last few core threads as for trailing by taking them through to the back and finish off neatly.

The finished example of tapered trailing.

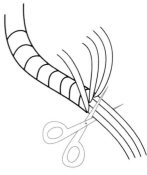

Diagram

DECORATIVE STITCHES

These stitches are useful for creating texture and different tones.
The following pages describe some of the most versatile stitches.

FRENCH KNOTS

French knots may be used in close clusters, or spaced out to give
different effects. For a first try I recommend coton à broder, but
French knots can be worked in any thread.

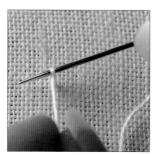

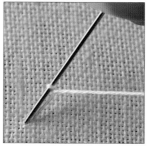

1 Bring the needle up, pull
through and wrap the thread once
round the needle.

2 Put the tip of the needle into
the fabric a tiny distance away,
still holding the thread wrapped
around the needle.

3 Pull the wrap down to the
bottom of the needle so that it
rests against the fabric.

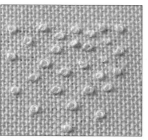

4 Pull the needle through to
complete the knot.

A group of French knots.

Diagram

SEEDING

Seeding is a nice way to create a gentle tone. It can be worked in various ways to create different looks. Experiment with different threads, patterns and stitch lengths.

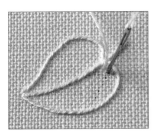

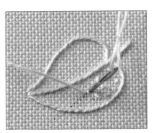

1 Surround a shape with an outline stitch; here I have used stem stitch. Make a tiny stitch in any direction inside the shape.

2 Continue making tiny stitches in the same way. They should be evenly spaced and all the same size.

This version of the stitch is known as random seeding.

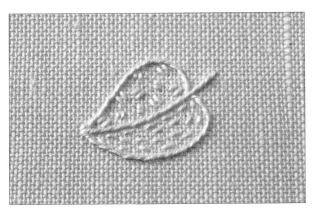

Here the lower part of the design is worked in directional seeding, where the stitches follow the curve of the shape. The top part is worked in double seeding, where the random stitches are worked in pairs.

STEM STITCH (OUTLINE STITCH)

Stem stitch (or outline stitch) is one of the most useful stitches, because it is so versatile and can be worked in any thread. It is a great line stitch that can handle any curve; and it can also be used as a filling stitch. Always keep the loop to the outside of the curve.

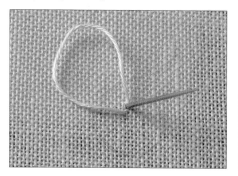

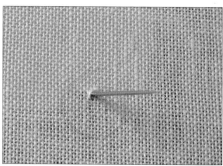

1 Bring the needle up at the end of the line and make a stitch about 3mm (¹/₈in) long, leaving a loop. Bring the needle up halfway along the first stitch and keep the needle resting in the fabric.

2 Pull the excess thread on the back to close the loop against the needle.

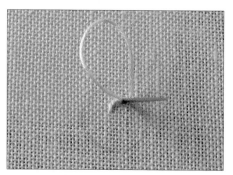

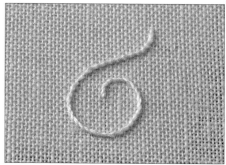

3 Make a new stitch the same length as the first, leaving a loop. Bring the needle up at the end of the first stitch and leave it resting in the fabric while you close the loop.

4 Repeat to the end of the line.

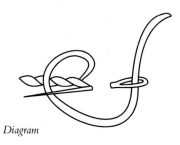

Diagram

FISHBONE STITCH

Fishbone stitch is a simple way to fill leaf, petal and fish shapes. It gives two distinct angles to catch the light and can be worked in any thread.

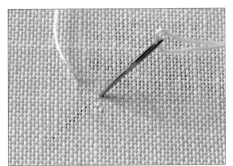

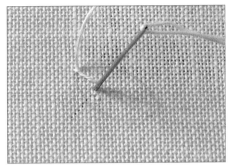

1 Starting from the tip of the leaf, make a stitch 5mm (¼in) down the centre line.

2 Bring the needle up on the outline, just to the right of the first stitch. Make a stitch, crossing over the end of the first stitch, finishing just to the left of the centre line.

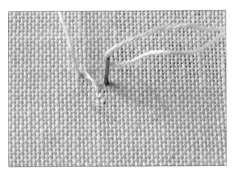

3 Bring the needle up on the outline, just to the left of the first stitch. Make a stitch, crossing over the end of the previous stitch, finishing just to the right of the centre line.

4 Continue to work in this way, moving down the shape until it is filled.

Diagram 1   *Diagram 2*   *Diagram 3*

COUNTED SATIN STITCH

Counted satin stitch is a good way to get an even pattern over a shape. It contrasts well with pulled thread work. There are endless patterns you can try; experiment with different threads and make up your own patterns. Use a tapestry needle so that it slides easily between the threads of the fabric.

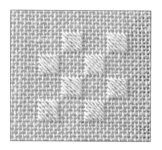

This pattern is made with square blocks of diagonal stitches, alternating with blank squares.

This pattern has alternating diagonal rows. Each row has pairs of either vertical or horizontal stitches. Two rows are worked with stranded cotton, then two with coton à broder and so on.

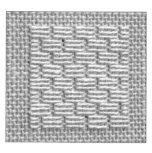

This pattern consists entirely of horizontal stitches over six threads. Blocks of three stitches are arranged in a bricked pattern.

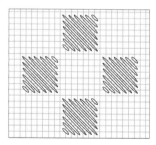

Diagram

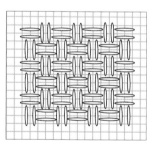

Diagram

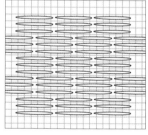

Diagram

Opposite

Dresden Work, RSN Collection. This piece of fine cloth is edged with a deep border, densely worked with a wide variety of pulled thread patterns and counted satin stitches.

EYELETS

Eyelets can be used to make beautiful designs with no other stitching, or just with satin stitch. This style of whitework is commonly known as Broderie Anglaise. They are also a useful addition to other designs.

EYELETS (ROUND)

Round eyelets are made by pushing the threads of the fabric apart, rather than cutting it; so they do not damage the fabric. They may be stitched with stranded cotton, coton à broder or perlé cotton.

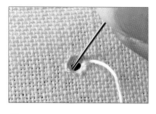

1 Work a ring of running stitch the desired size of the eyelet. The stitches should be about 2mm (¹⁄₈in) long. There is a limit to the size that can be made with this method – usually about 5mm (¼in). A single line of running stitch may be enough on fine fabric, but on coarse fabric I like to work double running stitch; go back around the ring filling in the gaps.

2 Push the tip of a stiletto into the centre of the ring, twisting the stiletto to increase the size of the hole gradually. Then remove the stiletto from the hole while you stitch.

3 Bring the needle up about 2mm (¹⁄₈in) outside the ring, and then pass the needle down through the hole. Bring the needle up again next to the first stitch and back through the hole again.

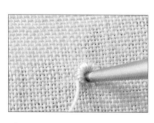

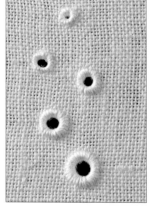

4 Repeat all the way around the eyelet, using the stiletto from time to time to neaten the hole.

5 Once complete, run the needle under a few stitches on the back to finish off tidily. Then use the stiletto to make sure the hole looks round.

A cluster of different sized eyelets stitched with this method. You can also make shaded eyelets by increasing the length of the stitches on one side.

SHAPED EYELETS

This method is used to create eyelets that are shaped (usually teardrop or leaf shaped) and may be used to create larger circular eyelets. They can be stitched with stranded cotton, coton à broder or perlé cotton.

1 Work a line of running stitch around the shape. The stitches should be about 2mm (¹/₈in) long. A single line of running stitch may be enough on fine fabric, but on coarse fabric I like to work double running stitch; go back around the shape filling in the gaps.

2 Insert the tip of a pair of very sharp embroidery scissors into the centre of the shape, and snip towards one end of the shape, being very careful not to cut your stitching.

3 Turn the scissors around and snip to the other end of the shape.

4 Carefully make two more cuts, from the middle to either side.

5 Gently fold each quarter of the fabric back underneath the surrounding fabric.

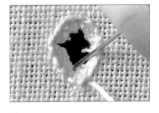

6 Bring the needle up about 2mm (¹/₈in) outside the running stitch line, and then pass the needle through the hole.

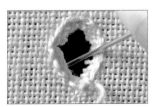

7 Bring the needle up again next to the first stitch and then back through the hole again.

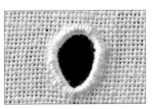

8 Continue all around the eyelet, trying to keep an even tension in the stitches and not distorting the fabric.

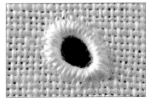

Try using a wider band of stitching for a bolder look.

DRAWN THREAD STITCHES

The essence of drawn thread work is the removal of threads from the fabric. This alone can create useful effects. Drawn thread stitches are perfect for borders, and also make pretty patterns that you can use to fill shapes. The following pages give you a step-by-step guide to drawn thread work.

PREPARATION

Before doing any drawn thread work, it is advisable to either remove your fabric from the frame entirely, or to loosen it so that it hangs slack in the frame. Then you can begin to remove threads. This method assumes that you are creating a border, or a line that does not meet any other stitching.

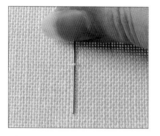

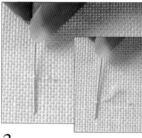

1 In the middle of the line you wish to remove, use a tapestry needle to hook up just one thread of the fabric and pull it up a little.

2 Slide the point of one blade of your embroidery scissors under the same thread, beside the needle, and snip the thread. It is very handy to have sharp-pointed curved scissors for this.

3 Move along the cut thread, using the needle to tease it free of the fabric. Continue this to the end of the line, and then do the same in the opposite direction.

4 Thread the needle with the unpicked thread and weave it back into the fabric by four or five threads to secure the end. Do the same at the other end. Do not cut the thread until all the necessary threads are removed, in case you need to adjust the tension. Then trim away all the excess thread.

This sample shows five drawn threads.

ALTERNATIVE PREPARATION

This method assumes that you are working your drawn thread up to other stitching. It works for any reasonably solid stitching including buttonhole stitch, satin stitch, close clustered French knots and trailing.

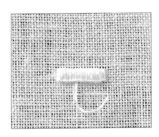

1 Before working your chosen stitch, work a line of double running stitch with lace thread, just inside the outline.

2 Work your chosen stitch along the line, covering the double running stitch. Here I have used buttonhole stitch (see page 78).

3 Remove the fabric from the frame and follow steps 1, 2 and 3 of the standard preparation.

4 Once all the necessary threads are unpicked right up to the stitching, lift them all up, away from the fabric and slide one blade of your embroidery scissors underneath. Move the scissors so that the flat of the blade rests against the stitching and carefully snip the threads. By ensuring that the flat of the blade is against the stitching, you reduce the risk of cutting through your stitches.

The finished preparation using buttonhole stitch.

You can also prepare for drawn thread work using French knots, as shown here.

Alternative preparation for drawn thread work using satin stitch.

HEM STITCH

Hem stitch is usually used to create a foundation for decorative stitches, but is an attractive stitch in its own right. It is very useful for borders, and may be worked on both sides of drawn threads, or just on one side for different effects. Vary the number of threads you gather together according to the look you want to achieve.

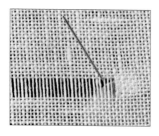 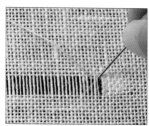 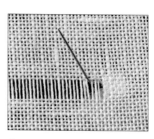

1 Cast on in the overwoven end, count three threads along and bring the needle up.

2 Go back over the same three threads and take the needle down.

3 Count three threads along and bring the needle up in the same place again.

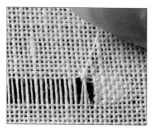  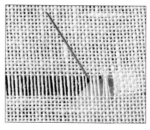

4 Pull the thread tight to draw the threads together.

5 Count into the fabric by two threads and take the needle down, while holding the thread tight. This acts as a holding stitch to keep the threads gathered.

6 Go back to the drawn threads and count three threads along. Bring the needle up ready for the next stitch. Continue all along one edge, then repeat on the other edge.

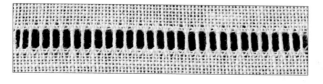

The finished sample of hem stitch.

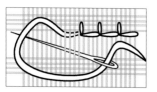 

Diagram 1   *Diagram 2*

DIAGONAL HEM STITCH

Diagonal hem stitch is a variant of hem stitch, using the same method. It gives you a simple diagonal pattern. For this variant, you need to gather an even number of threads; this sample shows four.

Work the first edge following the directions for hem stitch opposite but gathering four threads together. Then work the other edge with the same stitch, but staggering the gathering stitch by bringing the needle out just two threads along for the first stitch, and from then on gathering four threads together.

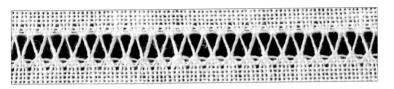

OVERCASTING

This is an alternative to hem stitch, giving a less dramatic effect. It is useful for very fine work where there may not be enough space for hem stitch, or as a quicker way to make a foundation for other stitches. It does not give quite such a strong edge as hem stitch, so it is not as practical for borders on household linens.

1 Cast on in the woven patch as before and come up in the first gap.

2 Put the needle down two threads along and two up into the linen.

3 Come up in the gap directly below.

The finished sample of overcasting. You need to pull fairly tightly to achieve the ladder effect.

DOUBLE TWIST

This is a great stitch for a reasonably wide border. For this sample, eight threads were removed, and then hem stitch was worked to gather the threads in bunches of two. This stitch can be tricky because it all relies on tension. Remember to keep holding the thread tightly all the way to the end and cast on and off very securely. Because it needs to be pulled so tight, it can be useful to work buttonhole stitch (page 78) over the overwoven ends before stitching.

1 Cast on in the overwoven end, count over four bunches and take the needle down.

2 Count back under two bunches and bring the needle up.

3 Count back over two bunches and take the needle down.

4 Count under four bunches and bring the needle up.

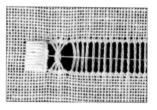

5 Pull the thread tight to twist the bunches together. Be careful to pull straight along the centre line so that the twist forms neatly.

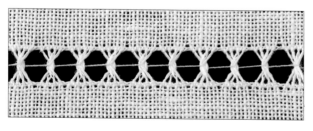

The finished sample of double twist.

70

Tulip

Worked by the author. The flower is stitched with pulled thread patterns. The background has a pattern of drawn threads throughout, and the piece is accented with trailing and padded satin stitch.

KNOTTED BORDER

This is a good stitch for almost any size of border. For this sample, eight threads were removed, and then hem stitch was worked to gather the threads in bunches of two. You could gather more threads, or stitch each knot over more bunches for different effects.

1 Bring the needle out in the first gap, loop the thread clockwise and take the needle back into the first gap.

2 Count under two threads and bring the needle up inside the loop.

3 Close the loop to make a knot.

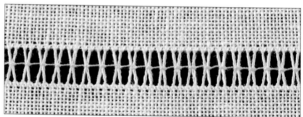

4 Pull tight. Continue in the same way.

The finished sample.

Opposite
Vogue

Worked by Helen Cox. This stunning contemporary piece shows the variation that can be achieved with whitework. It is perfectly suited to the defined straight lines in the text and border as well as the natural curves of the hair and flowers. The delicate drawn thread work in the background beautifully sets off the raised areas of satin stitch and long and short.

CHAIN

This is based on traditional chain stitch, but worked over drawn threads. It is lovely on narrow borders, but may also be repeated to fill a larger border. For this sample, five threads were removed.

1 Cast on in the overwoven end, count over two bunches and take the needle down.

2 Bring the needle up again in the first gap, below the first stitch.

3 Take the needle down in the first gap, above the first stitch, leaving a loop.

 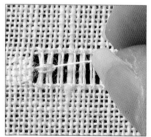

4 Count under two bunches and bring the needle up, inside the loop.

5 Pull through to close the chain. Remember this is a chain stitch rather than a knot, so do not pull too tight.

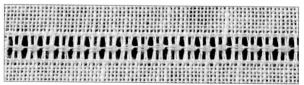

The finished sample.

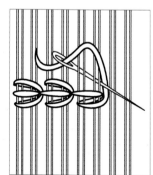

Diagram

WRAPPED BARS

Unusually for drawn thread work, this stitch uses stranded cotton.
The idea is to create small bars of satin stitch, rather than pull the
threads very tight.

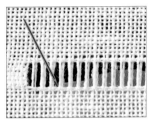

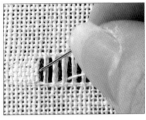

1 Cast on in the overwoven end, count under three bunches and bring the needle up.

2 Take the needle down in the first gap again.

3 Pull slightly to wrap the three bunches together, but not too tightly. Continue to wrap over the same bars, making sure that each wrap sits neatly next to the previous one. Push the wraps down with the needle to press them more tightly together.

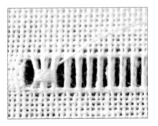

4 Continue to wrap the same way until you reach the other edge, then carry the thread under the next three bunches to start the next bar.

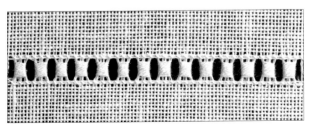

The finished example of wrapped bars.

DRAWN THREAD CORNERS

When working a border, you usually have a corner to fill. To prepare a corner,
follow the preparation steps (see page 66), making sure that the tension is even.
For a large corner I advise working a line of buttonhole stitch along each edge.

Buttonhole corner

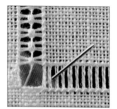 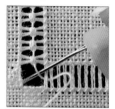 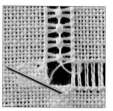 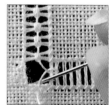

1 Work your chosen stitch down the length of the vertical border and with the same thread, begin the corner stitch. Bring the needle up two bunches into the horizontal border.

2 Take the needle down into the corner, catching the loop.

3 Bring the needle up two threads into the fabric.

4 Take the needle down into the corner, catching the loop.

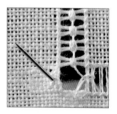 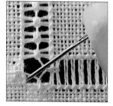 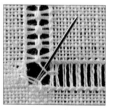 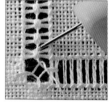

5 Bring the needle up two threads into the fabric.

6 Take the needle down into the corner, catching the loop.

7 Bring the needle up in the corner through the first loop.

8 To finish off neatly, take the needle down two bunches into the vertical border and run the needle through the stitching so that you can cast off on the edge.

 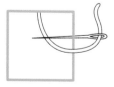

The finished buttonhole corner.

Diagram 1

Diagram 2. This stitch can be worked in either direction, so long as you catch each loop.

Woven wheel corner

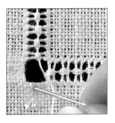 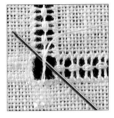 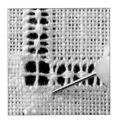 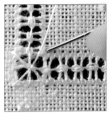

1 Work your chosen stitch down the length of the vertical border and then carry the thread across the corner, taking the needle two threads into the fabric opposite.

2 Use the needle to carefully wrap around the thread across the corner and then carefully run the needle through the stitching and cast off to the side. Repeat with the horizontal border.

3 Bring the needle up two threads into the fabric in the top left and take it down at the bottom right to form a diagonal stitch, then wrap around this thread back to the start. Make a couple of small stitches to travel to the bottom left.

4 Bring the needle up two threads into the fabric in the bottom left and pass the needle through the crossed threads in the centre before taking it down at the top right.

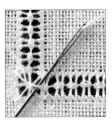  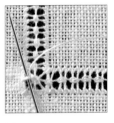 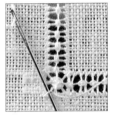

5 Wrap along the thread as far as the centre to complete the spokes of the wheel. Then begin to weave through the spokes.

6 Weave over and under alternate spokes all round the wheel, keeping the thread fairly tight the first time.

7 Weave round the wheel again, keeping the thread more relaxed for each subsequent circle so that it builds in size. Remember not to completely fill the corner.

8 After a few circles the wheel is complete. To finish off, wrap around the last spoke back to the bottom left and cast off in the fabric.

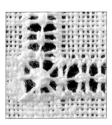 

The finished woven wheel corner.

Diagram

CUTWORK

Cutwork removes part of the fabric, allowing the backing material to show through. Buttonhole stitch is the traditional stitch used for cutwork, and is the easiest way to get a neat finish, because the stitch forms a corded edge. Stranded cotton and coton à broder work well for cutwork stitches. There are two methods to consider, depending on the shape you are stitching. For small, simple shapes such as circles, ovals or teardrops method 1 can be useful, because you trim the fabric first and fully encase the edge. For larger and more complex shapes method 2 gives a neat finish and can be used with buttonhole stitch, satin stitch or trailing. You can also use these methods to create a pretty hem for your work, for example a scalloped border. Work the stitches the other way round so that the corded edge faces outwards.

METHOD 1, BUTTONHOLE STITCH

This method must be worked after everything else is complete. It is worked on a still-tight frame, so you must be very careful with your tension. This method is best suited to very closely woven fabrics.

  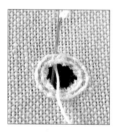 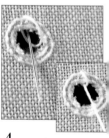

1 Work two lines of double running stitch around the shape and then begin to trim away the fabric by first cutting from the middle to each end, and then from the middle to each side.

2 Carefully trim each tab away and gently remove any fluff.

3 Cast on between the two running stitch lines. Bring the needle up through the hole and down just outside the outer line, leaving a loop.

4 Bring the needle up through the hole again, inside the loop. Pull through to complete the stitch and repeat all around the shape, making sure that the two ends match up neatly.

  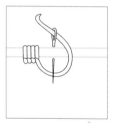

5 Cast off by running the needle under a few stitches on the back.

The finished example of cutwork with buttonhole stitch.

Diagram

Note

With this method you must be very careful with your tension. Pulling too tightly on the stitches can cause the fabric fibres to pull through the running stitch, ruining the shape.

METHOD 2

This may be worked with buttonhole stitch, satin stitch or trailing (see the examples on page 80). Here it is shown with basic, narrow buttonhole stitch, but you could also try a wider line of buttonhole stitch, in which case you may find it useful to stitch a line of split stitch under the outer edge, just as you would for satin stitch (see page 50). The stitching may be worked at the same time as other core stitches, but the cutting away should be done at the very end.

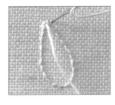

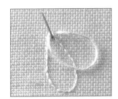

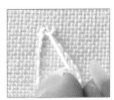

1 Work a line of double running stitch just outside the outline. To begin buttonhole stitch, bring the needle up just inside the line and take it down just outside the line, leaving a loop.

2 Bring the needle up just inside the line, right next to the first stitch, with the needle inside the loop.

3 Pull the excess thread to the back and then bring the needle and thread through to complete the stitch.

4 Repeat around the shape, placing the stitches as close together as you can. Make sure that the two ends match up neatly.

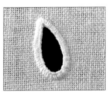

5 Begin to trim the fabric away by first cutting from the middle to each end, and then from the middle to each side.

6 Insert the scissors so that the flat of the blade rests against the stitches; this way the stitches will not be cut. Use small snipping movements to gradually trim away the fabric. Sometimes it is useful to turn to the back.

The finished example of cutwork with buttonhole stitch.

Note

To change thread while working, finish the last stitch by making a tiny stitch over the loop. Start a new thread and bring the needle up between the last two stitches to form the next loop.

BUTTONHOLE BARS

Buttonhole bars allow you to cut away larger shapes, by creating a network of supports. Consider whether you need these for support, and if they will add to the look of your design. Remember they really should be stitched before you do any cutting, not as an emergency fix afterwards!

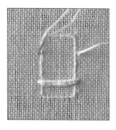  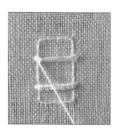 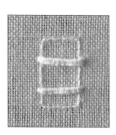

1 Bring the needle up on the right, just outside the running stitch, and down on the left. Make two more stitches: left to right, then right to left. The three threads across the gap should be taut, even a little too tight.

2 Bring the needle up on the left and begin to work buttonhole stitch across the three long stitches. Pass the needle eye-first under the threads from top to bottom, leaving a loop. Pass the needle over the loop.

3 Pull the thread tight to complete the stitch.

4 Repeat steps 2 and 3 across the bar, keeping the stitches close together and trying to keep an even tension. To finish the bar take the needle down outside the running stitch line. Work cutwork as before and be careful not to cut through the bars when you trim the fabric away.

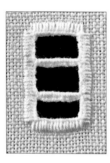

The finished example of buttonhole bars.

Note

It is really useful to have a pair of lace scissors for cutwork. They have a point on one blade and a ball on the other, so that you can slide between two layers easily.

SATIN STITCH

Work satin stitch in the same way as usual, following the steps on pages 50–53. Remember to work a line of double running stitch first.

TRAILING

Work trailing following the steps on page 56. I would advise keeping the trailing quite wide because it will be stronger, but it is possible to do this with narrow trailing on fine fabrics.

TAKING CARE OF YOUR EMBROIDERY

However you choose to display your embroidery, whether it is a functional item or a framed artwork, you want it to look its very best. Therefore it is important to know how to clean and store it. The following method of cleaning is appropriate for any textile (unless the colours run) and is a good way to clean historical or delicate embroidery. I have used an antique handkerchief from my collection to demonstrate. Once your embroidery is clean and dry, the best way to store it is wrapped in acid free tissue paper and/or a clean white cloth. If you are mounting your work for the wall, it will be best protected in a frame behind UV protective glass to prevent yellowing – and it really is best to wash the work before mounting.

WASHING YOUR WHITEWORK

1 Pour a little detergent into the bottom of a clean basin or container and fill with lukewarm water. Use detergent without optical brighteners if possible as these can leave residue. Place the embroidery on the surface, folded if necessary. Do not press down on the fabric.

2 Wait for the embroidery to sink naturally and leave for thirty minutes to one hour. If after this time any areas need particular attention, place the embroidery on a clean surface and use a very soft sponge to gently dab the area with the detergent solution.

3 Rinse the detergent out by soaking the embroidery the same way again in new, clean water. Repeat all steps if necessary.

Note

All embroidery looks darker when wet, so don't worry if it looks less than pristine during the cleaning process.

4 Once you are happy the embroidery is clean, remove it from the water and place it on a clean towel. If possible, open it out flat, but fold it if it is too big. Blot the embroidery with another clean towel laid flat on top. To reduce the need for pressing, open the embroidery out flat and pin it carefully to a folded towel. Insert pins along the edge of the piece and stretch the fabric just a little (not so much that the edge is distorted).

Using the stitches

The following pages guide you through a few of my designs, with details of the stitches used to achieve the effects. Hopefully this will help you think about your own designs and how to use the stitches you have learned.

BUTTERFLY

This design is based on a peacock butterfly (the design process is detailed on pages 22–23). I love butterflies, and they work beautifully in all types of embroidery. They have a natural symmetry that is very appealing to the eye, but you can see that the design, like a real butterfly, is not perfectly symmetrical. The butterfly is stitched on 32 TPI Edinburgh linen. The border has had a few threads drawn, and then hem stitch was worked along the inside edge only to achieve the pattern.

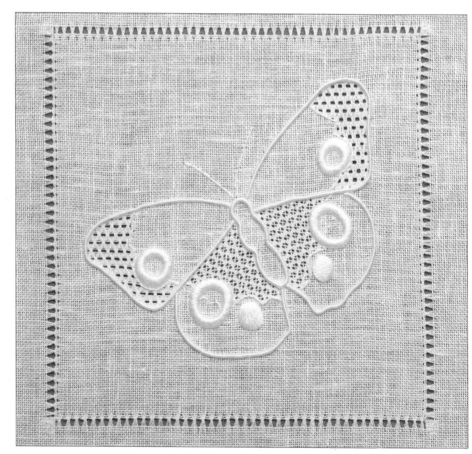

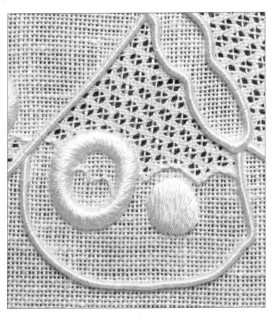

Detail of lower wing

Satin stitch is used here in two ways. The solid shape is worked with a single layer of satin stitch padding, then covered with basic satin stitch with stranded cotton. The circle is worked in turned satin stitch over varied depths of split stitch padding, which is perfect for this sort of shape because it can be turned easily around curves.

Detail of upper wing

The wings have three different pulled work patterns: diagonal drawn filling in the lower wings, wave stitch and honeycomb darning in the upper wings. The patterns were chosen to suit the shapes and to give a contrast. A fine lace thread was used so that it would almost disappear, emphasising the patterns.

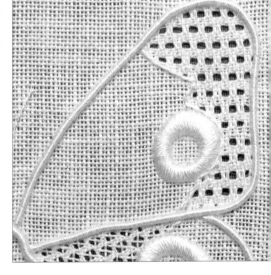

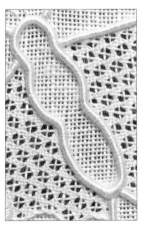

Detail of body

The body and wing outlines are worked in trailing. For the body, the two ends of trailing are neatly joined. The trailing is worked, leaving both ends of the core thread free until there is only a small gap left. Then the core threads are divided and taken through to the back slightly overlapped. The gap is then carefully stitched over so that no join can be seen.

Detail of bubbles

The bubbles and the fish's eye are all created
with round eyelets, using a stiletto. The lips
are two tiny shapes in satin stitch.

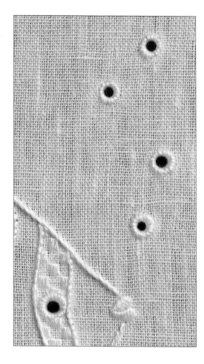

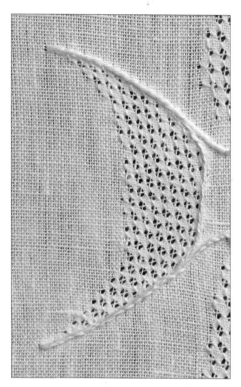

Detail of tail

The tail and fins are stitched with diagonal
drawn filling in two different sizes to give a little
variation. They are partly outlined with stem
stitch so that they blend into the body of the fish.
Where the stitches fade out into the background,
they are not outlined with double running stitch
– great care was taken to ensure the tension
around these areas remained even.

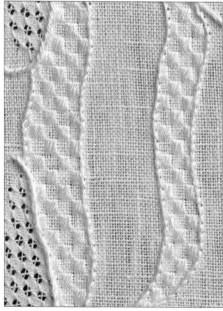

Detail of body

The stripes on the body are stitched with a counted
satin stitch pattern, and further emphasised by
outlines of double running stitch.

ANGELFISH

This contemporary design focuses on the use of simple methods to achieve results. Three main techniques are supplemented with outline stitches. The Angelfish is stitched on 55 TPI Kingston linen.

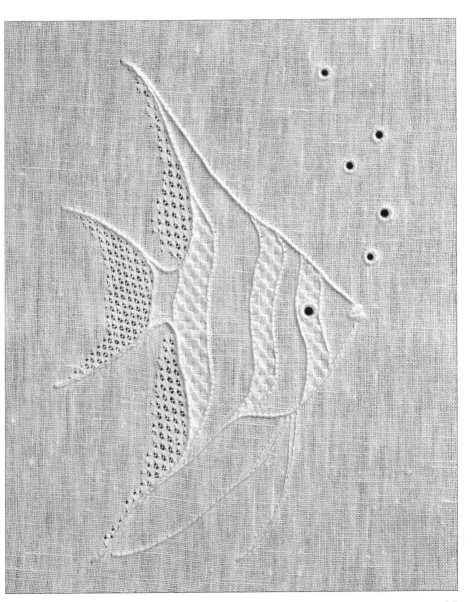

Moving on

REWORKING A TRADITIONAL DESIGN

I love approaching a project from a historical perspective, and there is so much antique whitework to be seen that the only hard part is which one to choose. By reworking a traditional design, I don't necessarily mean copying it stitch for stitch, although that can be an enjoyable process. In the following pages you will see how I have looked at an antique textile from the RSN Collection and taken inspiration from it to design my own embroidery.

This historical whitework, RSN Collection 27, is a length of fine cotton lawn embroidered with a repeated pattern of floral sprays and a geometric border. Though we have no record of what this piece was used for, it seems likely that it was intended to be a skirt panel or similar. It may date from the early 19th century.

I focused on this large flower as the starting point of my design. The petals are worked with a combination of pulled thread techniques, with dense stitching in fine coton à broder for the outlines.

The central petals are worked on an even finer fabric, with each petal being stitched separately and then cut out and applied to give a three-dimensional effect.

For this reworking I wanted to create a cleaner, modern and even more three-dimensional look while keeping the overall feel of the flower, so I decreased the number of petals and outlined each petal with turned, padded satin stitch using coton à broder. I added the circle border with trailing to ground the design.

I used two different combinations of pulled thread patterns to get variation through the flower. The first is diagonal drawn filling with diagonal cross filling (left); the second is single faggot stitch with diagonal drawn filling (right).

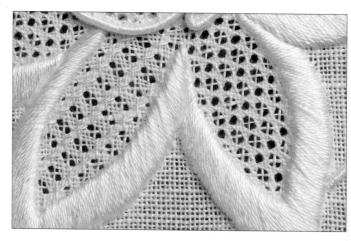

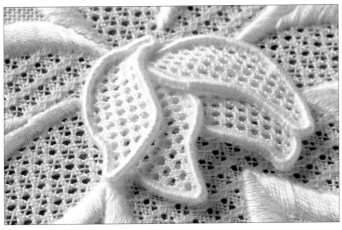

To create the central petals, I first drew each shape separately on a new piece of linen, and then filled each with single faggot stitch. I outlined them all with trailing, leaving the core threads trailing from the base of the petal. I then cut them out of the fabric, in the same way that you would for cutwork, and placed them on the design. I used the core threads to anchor the petals while stitching them in place, and then trimmed the excess away on the back.

The complete embroidery.

FURTHER TECHNIQUES

Once you have mastered all these stitches, you might like to explore further. The following pages give an introduction to layering fabrics and net embroidery.

USING LAYERS

Layering is a kind of upside down appliqué, which allows you to use a combination of different fabrics within a design. You might use one simply to create a shadow, or to show off different techniques. When planning your stitching, you must think about where you would like to position any extra layers. A layer of linen may be secured by any dense surface stitch, for example satin stitch or French knots, but a layer of net must have at least two lines of stitching to hold it – for example trailing plus a line of double running stitch. Net should be applied directly after working any pulled work areas. Linen should be applied partway through the embroidery, so that it is not trapped anywhere that is not necessary to secure it.

Here I have shown how to apply another layer of linen and a layer of net, which can be useful in lending a little support to a large cut area (this is most suitable for embroidery which will not take any strain, such as artwork). The fabric should be loose or in a slack frame while applying layers. First, cut a square of linen or net large enough to cover the required area, plus an extra inch or so all around.

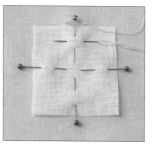 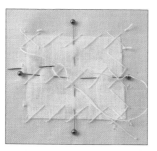 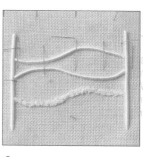

1 Turn to the back of the work. Pin the square to the main fabric as shown, lining up the straight grain. For a larger piece, use more pins, working from the centre out to the corners. With machine thread, use large basting stitches to secure the square, starting outside the square. Pass the needle through both layers, making a horizontal stitch underneath, and then repeat, leaving long diagonal stitches on the top.

2 Work a row of basting stitches through the middle and down both sides. For a larger piece, more lines will be needed; work these from the centre out to the sides. At the sides, the stitches should overlap the edge of the square. Then rotate the fabric and work lines in the opposite direction.

3 Work any stitching required to trap the layers. As you work, cut any basting threads that are in the way – do not stitch over them.

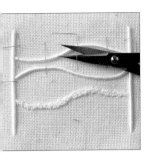

4 Once the stitching is complete, cut the remaining basting stitches and gently pull them away.

5 To trim the linen closely, first cut towards the stitching to create small tabs of fabric.

6 Carefully trim away each tab of fabric, keeping the flat of the blades against the stitches.

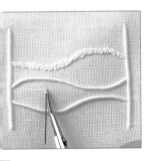
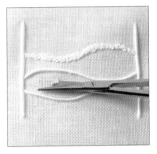

Note

It it is really useful to have a pair of lace scissors for cutwork. They have a point on one blade and a ball on the other, so that you can slide between two layers easily.

7 To remove the main linen over an area of net is a tricky task that really does require lace scissors. With a needle, make a small hole in the linen through which you can insert a scissor blade.

8 Once the hole is large enough insert the lace scissors, using the blade with the ball against the net. Carefully snip towards each end, create tabs as before and gently trim away the linen.

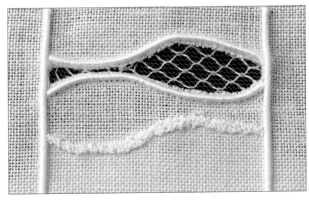

The finished layered piece.

NET DARNING

There are various methods of net embroidery; we are going to look at the simplest one, needlerunning, meaning simply that a needle is used to weave a pattern on the net.

When including a net layer, you can achieve some very pretty results with net embroidery. I have included three patterns for you to try, but you can experiment with many more of your own. You should use a small tapestry needle for net embroidery but you may use any type of thread provided that it fits comfortably through the holes in the net. Traditionally lace thread would be used but in these samples I have used stranded cotton for clarity.

The net embroidery must be completed before adding the layer to your main fabric, so make sure you have worked out the size of area you need to stitch, with 10mm (³⁄₈in) excess all around.

Casting on

Net darning is the only technique that has a different casting on method. Because there is no solid fabric, you must cast on with two half hitch knots.

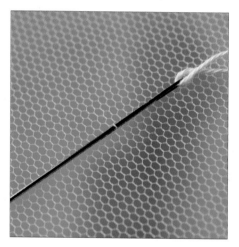

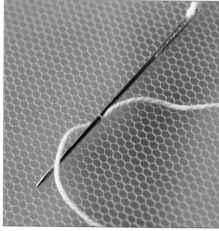

1 Pass the needle under one thread of the net, leaving a tail. Make sure it is a single thread rather than an intersection, so as not to distort the net.

2 Pass the needle under the same thread in the same direction as before, taking the needle through the loop of thread, and pull tight. It should catch in what is known as a half hitch knot.

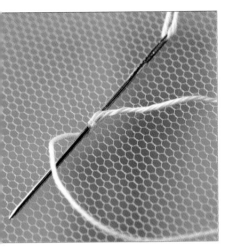

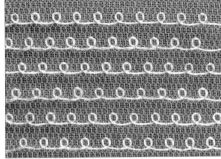

Net circles and (below) the diagram.

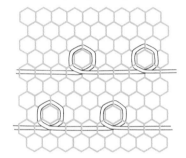

3 Repeat step 2, making sure you catch the loop again to form a second half hitch knot.

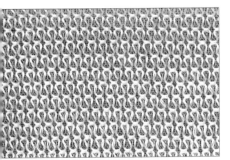

Net flowers and (below) the diagram.

Net waves and (below) the diagram.

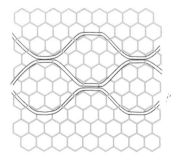

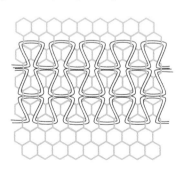

JAPANESE GARDEN

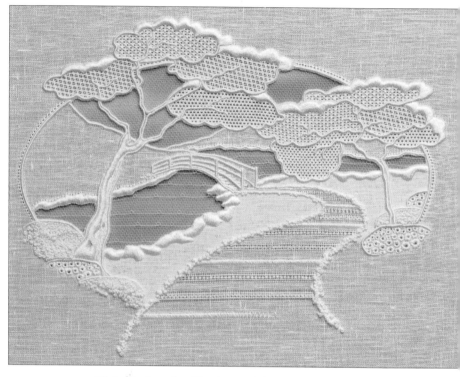

Worked by the author. This design includes all the types of technique shown in this book

Detail 1

The treetops are worked in various pulled thread patterns, using different gauges of lace thread to give contrast. The shapes are then outlined with trailing, flowing into turned satin stitch. Trailing has also been carefully worked over the net areas to create the branches.

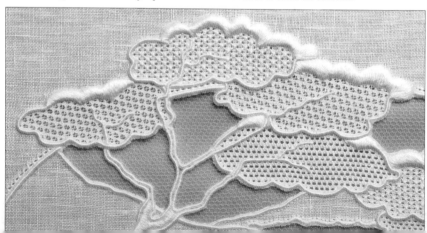

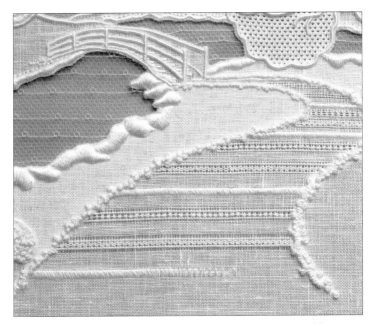

Detail 2

The pathway has been outlined with clustered French knots to represent pebbles, sealing the ends of the delicate drawn thread patterns. The boulders along the river's edge are individually worked in satin stitch at different angles to reflect the light. A very fine lace thread picks out movement in the river with a pattern of small circles.

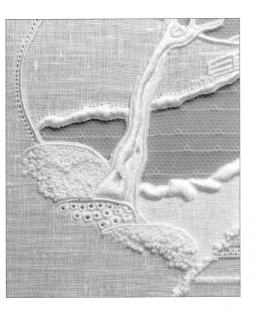

Detail 3

A combination of long and short, satin stitch and trailing make up the tree trunk, giving a three-dimensional look. The shrubs are outlined with trailing and filled with French knots and random pulled thread eyelets.

INDEX